# INTIMATE MOMENTS

## with

# THE FATHER

## Connecting with God
## in Mind and Heart

### GWEN EBNER

Path to Wholeness Publishing

*Intimate Moments with the Father: Connecting with God in*
   *Mind and Heart*
© 2016 by Path to Wholeness Publishing

Printed in the United States of America
ISBN 978-0-9981787-0-7

# *Lectio Divina*

While schools give students
hundreds of pages of text
and urge them to learn
speed reading,
(the person doing Lectio Divina)
dwells on a page or a passage
or a line for hours…. This method
allows reading to open,
not fill, our learning space.[1]

# CONTENTS

# PREFACE

This is the first book in a series called, "Seeds for your Spirit, Soul, and Body". It will assist you in connecting to God with both mind and heart though the practice of *Lectio Divina*. You can do *Lectio Divina* alone, with another person, or even in a small group.

**Chapter One** describes how to have a God Connection. **Chapter Two** explains the process of *Lectio Divina* and how to practice it. **Chapter Three** offers thirty sessions to help jumpstart your experience with *Lectio Divina*. Each session consists of a scripture, along with the four steps of Lectio Divina. Also, you will find space to journal your response, as well as a quote that relates to the scripture. **Chapter Four** gives you more scriptures for your *Lectio Divina* experience. The Appendices offer ideas for growing a more intimate relationship with God.

May God bless you as you listen to what he is saying each day. As you delight in his Word your desire to chew on Scripture day and night will grow. Then you will be like a tree "bearing fresh fruit every month, never dropping a leaf, always in blossom" (Ps. 1:3, MSG).

# INTRODUCTION

In 2001 I discovered the spiritual discipline of *Lectio Divina* and it has transformed the way I studied Scripture. In the past I had read the bible for information, which I found less intimidating.

In *Lectio Divina* you start reading the scripture using your mind, but then move to your heart. You close by applying God's Word to your everyday life. Now, you are able to have a two-way conversation with God as he reveals himself in surprising ways.

In 2004 God brought two women into my life that agreed to meet every week for Bible study. I suggested we do *Lectio Divina,* not realizing what an impact it would have on our lives! We have now met weekly for twelve years practicing *Lectio Divina* together. It is amazing how much we have grown through the experience! We have discovered that God speaks to each of us in a unique and different way and helps us change in many ways. We have supported and prayed for one another as God changed our hearts!

I would like you to hear what they have experienced as we did *Lectio Divina* together. Norma says:

> *Lectio Divina* has been an amazing way to study scripture with Connie and Gwen. We have established strong ties with each other through our times of vulnerability, openness, and honesty. Since

God speaks differently to each of us through scripture, we end up with a response specific to us. *Lectio Divina* is like someone opening a door into scripture and inviting us in. I have found each scripture meaningful for my own personal journey and the challenges I face. This method has provided a way for me to deeply examine a scripture, listening to God as he delivers the answer I need and the direction he wants me to take. Through my times in his presence, I have found the anchor I need to hang in there!

Connie also expressed her thoughts about *Lectio Divina*:

I felt a little awkward at first when Norma, Gwen, and I began to practice *Lectio Divina* in our bible study. I was unsure of what I was looking for and how to interpret the verses. Would I find the correct meaning? Would I reveal too much of myself? I found that even though our situations and needs were different, the verses spoke to each of our circumstances in unbelievable ways. I found this amazing to witness and experience! *Lectio Divina* is like looking at an ant with a microscope or gazing on a flower to see its finest detail. As we read the scripture we hear God speaking, guiding, ministering, advising, and directing. *Lectio Divina* keeps me in close communication with the Lord himself and becomes my direct line to God. It grows me, challenges my belief system, and helps me understand who God is. There are many ways to study the Word of God, but *Lectio Divina* has proven to be one of my favorites because I can hear God speaking to me specifically. I have allowed God to reach those closed off, dark corners of my heart. Through the practice of *Lectio Divina*, I can hear the prompting of the Holy Spirit, which allows God to become more alive than ever in my daily life!

One day as the three of us read Psalm 27, we realized that it described the process of *Lectio Divina*. "My heart has heard you say, 'Come and talk with me.' And my heart responds, 'Lord, I am coming'" (Ps. 27:8, NLT). *Lectio Divina* is definitely a tool that can lead us to God. Our part is to be available and willing to open our hearts to what he wants to say!

# CHAPTER 1

## FINDING A GOD CONNECTION

Do we not all long for a real God Connection? Listen to the Psalmist speak about his longing. "You, God, are my God, earnestly I seek you; I thirst for you, my whole being longs for you, in a dry and parched land where there is no water. I have seen you in the sanctuary and beheld your power and your glory. Because your love is better than life, my lips will glorify you" (Ps. 63:1-3). Did you hear his longing? he used phrases like, earnestly I seek you, I thirst for you, and your love is better than life.

God desires to connect with us. Jesus' sacrifice on the cross, opened the way to a direct line of communication with God. But how many of us have missed out on this incredible opportunity? The Psalmist in Psalm 63:1-3 had worked up a hunger and thirst for God and God's love was better than life. Maybe we lack that desire because we have an unending list of activities that keep us from even recognizing that we are hungry.

Could it be that the busyness of life steals our connection with God? Or maybe we get caught up in the trivial things of life instead of the urgent? Henri Nouwen, professor and priest, prayed this confession to God during a time of prayer. God, "I live as though there were something (more) important to be found outside of you".[2]

5

I believe the enemy prefers to get us caught up in hurry, noise, and crowds. Because when we rush, stay busy, and live with noise, we feel disconnected with God. The result is that we are unable to hear the gentle whisper of God's voice (I Kings 19:11-13).

"We need to recognize that all our much-doing is not always fruitful. It is sometimes mindless. Sometimes it is driven. It can be self-protecting. It keeps us going when in fact we should be still."[3] And isn't that the temptation we all experience in our lives? St. Augustine, an early Christian theologian, reminds us that God made us for himself, and our hearts are restless until we find our rest in him.[4]

During a time of deep struggle and searching, I began to find a real connection with God that I had never experienced. This connection happened as I learned how to spend time with God. This was a challenge for the adrenaline addict that I had become! This occurred when I found the practice of *Lectio Divina*, which engaged both my mind and heart as I reflected on scripture.

The practice of Lectio Divina finds its roots in the third century AD. with a man named Origins, an early Christian theologian. Later, in the Rule of St. Benedict, we discover a process for *Lectio Divina:* silence, the reading of scripture, and contemplation. Guigo II, a monk in the 12th century, formalized *Lectio Divina as* a four-step process.

Maggie and Duffy Robbins call *Lectio Divina* an Audience with the King. They believe this devotional practice can help us find "a practical way to listen and speak to the one who desperately wants a deeper relationship with us."[5]

In the practice of *Lectio Divina* "the Word that God speaks is alive and full of power…exposing and sifting and analyzing and judging the very thoughts and purposes of the heart" (Heb. 4:12, AMP). Have you ever experienced the Scripture speaking to your heart in that way? Are you allowing it to expose your thoughts and judge your heart? Are you applying it to your life as you read it? If you allow God to do this as you read his Word, it will result in amazing changes in your life!

*Lectio Divina* comes from two Latin words meaning divine reading. As we open our heart to the process of *Lectio Divina*, the Spirit gives us inner ears to hear the divine Word. "*Lectio Divina* is a personal prayer and each individual needs to see how it works best".[6]

It is also a process where one step leads into the next, helping us to draw closer to God. You can liken it to a tool shed next to the garden. It simply 'assists' us in cultivating the soil of our heart as we grow in Christ.[7]

Funk offers us this wisdom in regard to *Lectio Divina:*

> *Lectio Divina* is an appropriate way to read Scripture because God inspired these texts and there are many, many levels of meaning. Just as we have various physical senses…Scripture has various senses to help readers understand the meaning of the text and reveal its encounter with God….*Lectio*

*Divina* uses only two: the literal sense and the symbolic...sense.[8.]

The literal sense describes the use of our mind as we study and analyze the text. This takes place in the mind and helps us get the intended meaning of the writer. In contrast, the symbolic sense is the "meaning intended specifically for the prayerful reader...(which) occurs as we meditate and ponder, allowing the Holy Spirit to guide us with understanding."[9] This takes place in the heart and these two senses together allow *both* the mind and the heart to be involved in what God is saying to us.

Memorizing scripture is also helpful. "Write these commandments that I've given you today on your hearts. Get them inside of you and then get them inside your children" (Deut. 6:6). When you put God's Word in your heart, it is available to you at all times of your day.

It may seem more important to gain information from reading God's Word. But we must remember that *Lectio Divina* is not really about being informed but about hearing God speak to our hearts. We can read a lot of verses but if God is not revealed in and through the scripture, his Word will not become alive and active in us. We will finish our reading without having found out what God is saying to us and how we can respond.

Funk also reminds us that *Lectio Divina* is meant to be a way of living. In other words, we will understand the words only as we live them out in our lives. They become a yearning from the "deepest regions stored in our soul".[10]

Jesus confirmed this by saying, "Live in me. Make your home in me just as I do in you" (Jn. 15:4, MSG).

This method-less method of *Lectio Divina* is meant to be a free form, not a prescriptive practice. There is no particular amount of time assigned for each step. It will be different according to how the Spirit is speaking to you. Just "start reading and when you get to a hot spot stay and linger. Go wherever it takes you."[11]

The process of *Lectio Divina* moves in this manner: (1) reading of the word (gentle listening that helps us become focused); (2) meditation (pondering on God's words as we consider the meaning); (3) prayer (a response to God from a listening heart); and (4) contemplation (resting in God).

*Lectio Divina* is most helpful when done with both mind and heart. This means we involve both dimensions of the brain, left and right. "A person who is left-brained is often said to be more logical, analytical and objective, which tends to influence language, logic, critical thinking, numbers, reasoning, and even right hand control."[12]

On the other hand, "a person who is right-brained is said to be more intuitive, thoughtful and subjective."[13] This involves images, reading emotions, color, music, intuition/insight, holistic thought, imagination, creativity,[14] and left hand control.

If we only involve the left-brain, we will tend to stay at the informational and analytical level. But when we reflect and meditate, using our imagination and senses, we begin to access our right brain. This allows time for the Spirit to speak to us, as we reflect with both our heart and soul.

Hearing God's voice, which engages one of the senses likely takes place in the right hemisphere of the brain. Sometimes people with careers that seem more left-brained[15] say they struggle hearing God's voice. But they may feel uncomfortable with the right brain functions because they are more used to using their left-brain function.

God created everyone with the ability to access and use both the mind and heart. Jesus even instructs us to involve both mind and heart in our relationship with God. "Love the Lord your God with all your heart and with all your soul and with all your mind" (Matt. 22:37). A number of other scriptures instruct us in using our heart as well (Deut. 30:14, 32:46; Psa. 49:3, Psa. 119:34; Prov. 23:12; Rom. 10:8; Heb. 8:10).

Yet habits are not changed overnight; they take practice. Routines like rushing, busyness, and the desire for control tend to shut down right-brain processes. And once we access adrenaline from so much activity, it becomes difficult to be silent and still. This is exactly what the enemy prefers so that we have difficulty hearing God's voice and sensing his presence!

The authors of Scripture speak often about meditation. "The Bible uses two different Hebrew words to convey the idea of meditation and together they are used some fifty-eight times."[16] This indicates that listening, reflecting, and ruminating on God's Word is an important practice according to Scripture.

As we meditate we develop "a familiar friendship with Jesus."[17] The Scripture becomes a joyful experience instead of something we have to read. "We create the emotional and spiritual space which allows Christ to construct an inner sanctuary in the heart".[18]

So how do we meditate with the heart? "The devotional masters of nearly all persuasions counsel us that we can descend with the mind into the heart most easily through the imagination.... Our imagination helps to anchor our thoughts and focus our attention."[19] Jesus himself often taught in parables, "making constant appeal to the imagination"[20]

Some Christians have a problem with using the imagination believing it is untrustworthy and easily used by the enemy. "But just as we can believe that God can take our reason (fallen as it is)...and use it for his good purposes, so can God sanctify the imagination and use it for his good purposes."[21]

A.W. Tozer agrees with the use of imagination too. "I long to see the imagination released from its prison and given its proper place among the Sons of the new creation." [22] As we use our imagination, we will begin to see ourselves in the scene. We will visualize ourselves as the person in the biblical story. We will hear Jesus' words as if said just for us. We will feel the emotions of the story as well as our own. And we will sense how God wants us to apply the words to our own life. Yes, God wants to use our minds, but also our emotions, senses, and even our imagination as we read his word.

After the birth of Jesus and the Wise men's visit, Luke says, "Mary kept all these things [in her **mind**], pondering [them] in her **heart**" (Luke 2:19, DBY, bold added). May we too use both our mind and heart as we meditate on God's Word.[23]

# Chapter 2

# The Practice of *Lectio Divina*

The purpose of *Lectio Divina* is to engage the mind and then move the heart to devotion. This occurs when we take the time to read Scripture slowly, meditatively, and a number of times. This helps draw out meaning from the passage we are reading. Guerrique d'Igny compares the process of *Lectio Divina* to the process of a bee drawing honey from a flower. [24] We find the treasure God has for us as we linger and reflect on the words.

Guigo's four rungs of the ladder of *Lectio Divina* contain these steps: Reading (Lectio Divina), Meditation (meditatio), Prayer (oratio), and Contemplation (contemplatio). Through *Lectio Divina* God is "made known to us, speaks to us, and shapes our lives".[25] Dom Marmion describes the steps of *Lectio Divina* this way, "We read *(Lectio Divina)* under the eye of God *(meditatio)* until the heart is touched *(oratio)* and leaps to flame *(contemplatio)*".[26]

We tend to make the reading of scripture an intellectual exercise. That's why the second step of *Lectio Divina* moves us to meditation, which takes place in our inner intellect (our heart). In the third step *Lectio Divina* operates at the level of desire, offering us an opportunity to respond to God's words.

Since *Lectio Divina* is a free form, method-less method, it will take its own form each time. Do not try to confine God to a set method; allow him to work in you as he chooses. Some days you may spend more time on one part of *Lectio Divina* than the others. Allow the Spirit to direct you in this.

There are a number of ways to practice *Lectio Divina* but this is the basic form that I have used myself:

Begin with a time of silence to quiet your heart. This can happen through cleansing breaths, body relaxation, visualizing God within you or you with God, use of calming herbs and relaxing teas, lighting a candle, or listening to wordless music. (See Appendix A for more ideas on quieting your heart.) Then in prayer acknowledge God's presence and your desire for his guidance.

After that, move to the four steps of *Lectio Divina:*

- *Lectio Divina*: Read a brief portion of Scripture slowly several times, listening for a key word or phrase. If you are doing this alone, read the Scripture out loud. Michael Casey calls this active reading.[27]

- *Meditatio:* Meditate, reflecting on the Scripture, especially the word or phrase that spoke to you the most. As you attend to the deeper meanings of the text, pay attention to the emotions that surface in you.

This is a time of listening and reflecting in order to allow the words to sink from your head to your heart. Meditation can be compared to the process of a cow chewing its cud. Since it has four stomachs it chews and re-chews a number of times!

Casey reminds us to slow down and savor what we read in order to allow the text to trigger memories and associations that reside below the threshold of our awareness.[28]

- *Oratio:* Even though *Lectio Divina* is a free-style prayer, it can be helpful to ask God for illumination. Why has the word and emotions been evoked in me? As you continue listening, God will guide you on how to apply it.

Thom Gardner suggests that this can also be a step for Restoring. In that respect we ask God, "Why do these words or phrase stand out to me? Why do these emotions stir me?" And thirdly, "Is there anything, Lord, you want to heal in me"?[29]

- *Contemplatio:* A period of silence is kept in order to rest in God and in what he has said to you. This is a step of not only resting but also becoming. This, however, will be a continuous process even after you end this formal time of *Lectio Divina*.

You may notice that the method of *Lectio Divina* includes moments of reading (Lectio Divina), reflecting on (meditatio), responding to (oratio) and resting in (contemplatio) the Word of God with the aim of nourishing and deepening one's relationship with God.[30]

A simple word of Warning: Since *Lectio Divina* is a spiritual discipline that can draw you closer to God and allow you to prayerfully dialogue with him, don't be surprised when you find yourself distracted. The enemy loves to sidetrack us from spending meaningful time with God!

Also, be aware that each person approaches Scripture from their own perception – how they see God, the hurts they have experienced, what they have been taught in the past, etc. That is why it is important at the beginning of *Lectio Divina* to ask the Holy Spirit to direct your thoughts and guide your time in the Word. This is another reason I love doing it with others. Since they see things from their own viewpoint, they can provide a safeguard for misinterpretation.

If you want to try Group *Lectio Divina*, here is a brief outline suggested by Tony Jones:[31]

- After you quiet your heart and pray a short prayer acknowledging God's presence, the passage is read two or three times, slowly and deliberately. The group is asked to consider a word or phrase that speaks to them. *They can then share this with the group.*

- The scripture is read again two times (possibly in a different translation) and the group is encouraged to notice the emotions or feelings that surface in them. *They can share what they experience with the group.*
- The scripture is read again with a longer period of silence. During the silence they ask God why he brought the word or feeling to their attention and how he wants them to apply it to their life. *A time of sharing takes place as they share what God is saying to them through the Scripture.* The session ends in silent prayer or prayer for each other.

## PREPARING FOR *LECTIO DIVINA*

First, set aside a time of your day for doing *Lectio Divina.* Second, be aware that the tone of your day will be crucial in preparing you for *Lectio Divina.* "If we are constantly being swept off our feet with frantic activity, we will be unable to be attentive at the moment of inward silence".[32] Lectio Divina will be most helpful when you have a sense of balance in your life and a peaceful spirit. This can happen as we purposefully make an effort to connect with God regularly throughout the day, attempt to walk, talk, and drive slower, and purpose to live with a prayerful heart.

When practicing *Lectio Divina*, it might be helpful to have read from several different translations. This is not necessary since you can use only one version if you prefer.

Saint Benedict described *Lectio Divina* as "cultivating the ability to listen deeply (and) to hear 'with the ear of our heart'".[33] In order to do this it will be helpful to find a quiet place to read that is free from distractions so that it can become your meeting place with God. It will also be important to turn off your cell phone, computer, and other media that may distract you from hearing God's voice. As you begin *Lectio Divina*, take time to quiet your heart.

More important than what *Lectio Divina* is and how we do it, is that we do it. Chapter Three will give you an opportunity to practice *Lectio Divina* for 30 days. Then you will have the opportunity to choose whether to continue using it as a way of living.

# CHAPTER 3

# 30 DAYS OF PRACTICING *LECTIO DIVINA*

Chapter Three offers you a format for practicing *Lectio Divina* for the next 30 days. In this chapter you will find:

1. A suggested scripture for the day
2. Some background understanding about the scripture
3. The four steps of *Lectio Divina* with a blank space after each step so that you can interact with the scripture [Once you have recorded your responses in writing, a journal record will be available of what God has said to you]
4. Each day will conclude with a quote that connects with the theme of the scripture

# Day One

**Scripture:** Philippians 4:4-7

**Background**: Paul is in prison when he writes this letter to the church at Philippi. He advises them to work together (verses 2-3) and then instructs them in their responses to life. [Take a few moments to scan through the whole chapter in order to be aware of the context and setting of the text before you begin.]

**The Four Steps of *Lectio Divina*:**

1. *Lectio* (read): [Spend a few moments quieting your heart; then prayerfully acknowledge God's presence.] Read the passage out loud 2-3 times slowly. *What is the word or phrase that stands out to you in this passage?*_____
   _____
   _____

2. *Meditatio* (meditate): Reread the passage slowly in the same or different version. [As you attend to the deeper meaning of the text, pay attention to the feelings and emotions that arise in you. Allow your imagination & senses to be involved as well.] *What did you experience and observe?*_____
   _____
   _____
   _____
   _____

3. *Oratio* (prayer): Reread the passage one more time. Actively listen and converse with God about the meaning and application of the scripture. [Ask God why this particular word/phrase and emotions is being evoked in you.] *What did you sense God saying and how does he want to respond?*

_____

_____

_____

_____

_____

4. *Contemplatio* (contemplation): A period of silence is kept in order to rest in God. *[End with a prayer of commitment to what you have heard God say. Feel free to speak your prayer or to write it out.]* _____

_____

_____

_____

_____

_____

*Have you heard of the cushion of the sea? Down beneath the surface that is agitated by storms, and driven about with winds, there is a part of the sea that is never stirred.... The peace of God is that eternal calm which, like the cushion of the sea, lies far too deep down to be reached by any external trouble and disturbance; and those who enter into the presence of God become partakers of that undisturbed and undisturbable calm.*

~ L.B. Cowman, from Streams in the Desert

# Day Two

**Scripture:** Psalm 63:1-8

**Background**: David is on his way to the wilderness of Judah, his enforced exile. Even though his political fortunes are at a low ebb, his spiritual vitality is high. [Take a few moments to scan through the whole chapter in order to be aware of the context and setting of the text before you begin.]

**The Four Steps of *Lectio Divina*:**

1. *Lectio* (read): [Spend a few moments quieting your heart; then prayerfully acknowledge God's presence.] Read the passage out loud 2-3 times slowly. *What is the word or phrase that stands out to you in this passage?*_____

   _____

   _____

2. *Meditatio* (meditate): Reread the passage slowly in the same or different version. [As you attend to the deeper meaning of the text, pay attention to the feelings and emotions that arise in you. Allow your imagination & senses to be involved as well.] *What did you experience and observe?*_____

   _____

   _____

   _____

   _____

22

3. *Oratio* (prayer): Reread the passage one more time. Actively listen and converse with God about the meaning and application of the scripture. [Ask God why this particular word/phrase and emotions is being evoked in you.] *What did you sense God saying and how does he want to respond?*

_____

_____

_____

_____

_____

4. *Contemplatio* (contemplation): A period of silence is kept in order to rest in God. *[End with a prayer of commitment to what you have heard God say. Feel free to speak your prayer or to write it out.]* _____

_____

_____

_____

_____

_____

*O God, I have tasted Thy goodness, and it has both satisfied me and made me thirsty for more. I am painfully conscious of my need for further grace. I am ashamed of my lack of desire. O God, the Triune God, I want to want Thee; I long to be filled with longing; I thirst to be made more thirsty still. Show me Thy glory, I pray Thee, so that I may know Thee indeed. Begin in mercy a new work of love within me.*
~ A.W. Tozer

# Day Three

**Scripture:** Exodus 14:10-14

**Background:** The Israelites are encamped near the Red Sea and seemingly trapped as they see Pharaoh and his army overtaking them. They are now between the devil (Pharaoh) and the deep blue (Red) sea. [Take a few moments to scan through the whole chapter in order to be aware of the context and setting of the text before you begin.]

**The Four Steps of *Lectio Divina*:**

1. *Lectio* (read): [Spend a few moments quieting your heart; then prayerfully acknowledge God's presence.] Read the passage out loud 2-3 times slowly. *What is the word or phrase that stands out to you in this passage?*_____
   _____
   _____

2. *Meditatio* (meditate): Reread the passage slowly in the same or different version. [As you attend to the deeper meaning of the text, pay attention to the feelings and emotions that arise in you. Allow your imagination & senses to be involved as well.] *What did you experience and observe?*_____
   _____
   _____
   _____
   _____

5. *Oratio* (prayer): Reread the passage one more time. Actively listen and converse with God about the meaning and application of the scripture. [Ask God why this particular word/phrase and emotions is being evoked in you.] *What did you sense God saying and how does he want to respond?*

_____

_____

_____

_____

_____

_____

6. *Contemplatio* (contemplation): A period of silence is kept in order to rest in God. *[End with a prayer of commitment to what you have heard God say. Feel free to speak your prayer or to write it out.]* _____

_____

_____

_____

_____

*Be silent, and listen to God.*
*Let your heart be in such a state of preparation*
*that his Spirit may impress upon you*
*such virtues as will please him.*
*Let all within you listen to him.*
*This silence of all outward and earthly affection*
*and of human thoughts within us*
*is essential if we are to hear his voice.*
~ Francois Fénelon

25

# Day Four

**Scripture:** Psalm 16:5-11

**Background**: David did not do anything to provoke the current hostility of his foes but, in trust, is committing his cause to God and keeping his eyes on him instead of the situation. [Take a few moments to scan through the whole chapter in order to be aware of the context and setting of the text before you begin.]

**The Four Steps of *Lectio Divina*:**

1. *Lectio* (read): [Spend a few moments quieting your heart; then prayerfully acknowledge God's presence.] Read the passage out loud 2-3 times slowly. *What is the word or phrase that stands out to you in this passage?*_____

   _____

   _____

2. *Meditatio* (meditate): Reread the passage slowly in the same or different version. [As you attend to the deeper meaning of the text, pay attention to the feelings and emotions that arise in you. Allow your imagination & senses to be involved as well.] *What did you experience and observe?*_____

   _____

   _____

   _____

   _____

3. *Oratio* (prayer): Reread the passage one more time. Actively listen and converse with God about the meaning and application of the scripture. [Ask God why this particular word/phrase and emotions is being evoked in you.] *What did you sense God saying and how does he want to respond?*

_____

_____

_____

_____

_____

4. *Contemplatio* (contemplation): A period of silence is kept in order to rest in God. *[End with a prayer of commitment to what you have heard God say. Feel free to speak your prayer or to write it out.]* _____

_____

_____

_____

_____

*Reliance on God results in abundant living because it is the way we were designed to live...dependent on him. The essence of Adam and Eve's first sin was their desire to be like God and thus capable of living independently. Ever since then, depending on God continually has gone against the grain of human nature...The more frequently you look to him for help, the more you will find him faithful...Awareness of your neediness is actually a rich blessing – connecting you to him and his abundant supply!*
~ Sarah Young

# Day Five

**Scripture:** Psalm 1:1-6

**Background**: This Psalm dispels the common illusion that the sinful life will bring true and lasting satisfaction. Instead we are given a picture of the person who is truly blessed. [Take a few moments to scan through the whole chapter in order to be aware of the context and setting of the text before you begin.]

**The Four Steps of *Lectio Divina*:**

1. *Lectio* (read): [Spend a few moments quieting your heart; then prayerfully acknowledge God's presence.] Read the passage out loud 2-3 times slowly. *What is the word or phrase that stands out to you in this passage?*_____

   _____

   _____

2. *Meditatio* (meditate): Reread the passage slowly in the same or different version. [As you attend to the deeper meaning of the text, pay attention to the feelings and emotions that arise in you. Allow your imagination & senses to be involved as well.] *What did you experience and observe?*_____

   _____

   _____

   _____

   _____

3. *Oratio* (prayer): Reread the passage one more time. Actively listen and converse with God about the meaning and application of the scripture. [Ask God why this particular word/phrase and emotions is being evoked in you.] *What did you sense God saying and how does he want to respond?*

_____

_____

_____

_____

4. *Contemplatio* (contemplation): A period of silence is kept in order to rest in God. *[End with a prayer of commitment to what you have heard God say. Feel free to speak your prayer or to write it out.]* _____

_____

_____

*Christian meditation must not be confused with yoga, Eastern meditation or transcendental meditation. For, unlike these disciplines, Christian meditation has nothing to do with emptying our minds…it engages every part of us – our mind, our emotions, our imagination, our creativity and, supremely, our will…it involves, not emptiness, but fullness. It means being attentive to God. The purpose of this attentiveness, this reflecting and this pondering is, among other things, to see ourselves in the light of God's revealed word….We meditate to give God's words the opportunity to penetrate, not just our minds, but our emotions – the places where we hurt – and our will – the place where we make choices and decisions. We meditate to encounter the Living Word, Jesus himself.*
~ Joyce Huggett

# Day Six

**Scripture:** Joshua 1: 5-9

**Background:** The book of Joshua is the story of God leading his people into the Promised Land. Moses has died and God is now preparing Joshua as the new leader for this task. [Take a few moments to scan through the whole chapter in order to be aware of the context and setting of the text before you begin.]

**The Four Steps of *Lectio Divina*:**

1. *Lectio* (read): [Spend a few moments quieting your heart; then prayerfully acknowledge God's presence.] Read the passage out loud 2-3 times slowly. *What is the word or phrase that stands out to you in this passage?*_____

   _____

   _____

2. *Meditatio* (meditate): Reread the passage slowly in the same or different version. [As you attend to the deeper meaning of the text, pay attention to the feelings and emotions that arise in you. Allow your imagination & senses to be involved as well.] *What did you experience and observe?*_____

   _____

   _____

   _____

   _____

   _____

3. *Oratio* (prayer): Reread the passage one more time. Actively listen and converse with God about the meaning and application of the scripture. [Ask God why this particular word/phrase and emotions is being evoked in you.] *What did you sense God saying and how does he want to respond?*

_____

_____

_____

_____

_____

_____

4. *Contemplatio* (contemplation): A period of silence is kept in order to rest in God. *[End with a prayer of commitment to what you have heard God say. Feel free to speak your prayer or to write it out.]* _____

_____

_____

_____

_____

*Beloved, I say, let your fears go, lest they make you fainthearted. Stop inspiring fear in those around you and now take your stand in faith. God has been good and he will continue to manifest his goodness........ Let us approach these days expecting to see the goodness of the Lord manifest. Let us be strong and of good courage, for the Lord will fight for us if we stand in faith.*
~ Francis Frangipane

# Day Seven

**Scripture:** Mark 8:27-38

**Background:** Peter has just proclaimed who Jesus is, the Messiah, and Jesus reveals to his disciples what that will mean. He invites the crowd to join his disciples in following him, describing the cost it will involve. [Take a few moments to scan through the whole chapter in order to be aware of the context and setting of the text before you begin.]

## The Four Steps of *Lectio Divina*:

1. *Lectio* (read): [Spend a few moments quieting your heart; then prayerfully acknowledge God's presence.] Read the passage out loud 2-3 times slowly. *What is the word or phrase that stands out to you in this passage?*_____
   _____
   _____

2. *Meditatio* (meditate): Reread the passage slowly in the same or different version. [As you attend to the deeper meaning of the text, pay attention to the feelings and emotions that arise in you. Allow your imagination & senses to be involved as well.] *What did you experience and observe?*_____
   _____
   _____
   _____

32

3. *Oratio* (prayer): Reread the passage one more time. Actively listen and converse with God about the meaning and application of the scripture. [Ask God why this particular word/phrase and emotions is being evoked in you.] *What did you sense God saying and how does he want to respond?*

_____

_____

_____

_____

_____

_____

4. *Contemplatio* (contemplation): A period of silence is kept in order to rest in God. *[End with a prayer of commitment to what you have heard God say. Feel free to speak your prayer or to write it out.]* _____

_____

_____

_____

_____

*We imagine that self-denial most certainly means the rejection of our individuality....On the contrary, Jesus called us to self-denial without self-hatred. Self-denial is simply a way of coming to understand that we do not have to have our own way...getting what we want....Self-denial does not mean the loss of our identity...(and) is not the same thing as self-contempt. Self-contempt claims that we have no worth....Self-denial declares that we are of infinite worth and shows us how to realize it.*
~ Richard Foster

# Day Eight

**Scripture:** Psalm 46:1-7

**Background:** It is thought that the background of this Psalm is the miraculous deliverance of Jerusalem when besieged by Sennacherib. The people of Judah are conscious of God's presence with them and are celebrating the praises of God who is with them. [Take a few moments to scan through the whole chapter in order to be aware of the context and setting of the text before you begin.]

**The Four Steps of *Lectio Divina*:**

1. *Lectio* (read): [Spend a few moments quieting your heart; then prayerfully acknowledge God's presence.] Read the passage out loud 2-3 times slowly. *What is the word or phrase that stands out to you in this passage?*_____

    _____

    _____

2. *Meditatio* (meditate): Reread the passage slowly in the same or different version. [As you attend to the deeper meaning of the text, pay attention to the feelings and emotions that arise in you. Allow your imagination & senses to be involved as well.] *What did you experience and observe?*_____

    _____

    _____

    _____

    _____

3. **Oratio** (prayer): Reread the passage one more time. Actively listen and converse with God about the meaning and application of the scripture. [Ask God why this particular word/phrase and emotions is being evoked in you.] *What did you sense God saying and how does he want to respond?*

_____

_____

_____

_____

4. **Contemplatio** (contemplation): A period of silence is kept in order to rest in God. *[End with a prayer of commitment to what you have heard God say. Feel free to speak your prayer or to write it out.]* _____

_____

_____

_____

*Belief is confidence placed in the truth of what God has revealed to us in Scripture about who he is and our relationship to him through Jesus. Belief does not hover aimlessly in mid-air, but plants itself in the firm foundation of inspired, revelatory words inscripturated for us in the Bible.* ~ Sam Storms

*Oh, how great peace and quietness would he possess who should cut off all vain anxiety and place all his confidence in God.*
~ Thomas à Kempis

# Day Nine

**Scripture:** Deuteronomy 11:13-21

**Background**: Since the Israelites are soon to enter the Promised Land, Moses restates the law for the new generation that has arisen during the wilderness journey. [Take a few moments to scan through the whole chapter in order to be aware of the context and setting of the text before you begin.]

**The Four Steps of** *Lectio Divina*:

1. *Lectio* (read): [Spend a few moments quieting your heart; then prayerfully acknowledge God's presence.] Read the passage out loud 2-3 times slowly. *What is the word or phrase that stands out to you in this passage?*_____

_____

_____

2. *Meditatio* (meditate): Reread the passage slowly in the same or different version. [As you attend to the deeper meaning of the text, pay attention to the feelings and emotions that arise in you. Allow your imagination & senses to be involved as well.] *What did you experience and observe?*_____

_____

_____

_____

_____

_____

3. *Oratio* (prayer): Reread the passage one more time. Actively listen and converse with God about the meaning and application of the scripture. [Ask God why this particular word/phrase and emotions is being evoked in you.] *What did you sense God saying and how does he want to respond?*

_____

_____

_____

_____

_____

_____

4. *Contemplatio* (contemplation): A period of silence is kept in order to rest in God. *[End with a prayer of commitment to what you have heard God say. Feel free to speak your prayer or to write it out.]* _____

_____

_____

_____

*And these will be the signs of God being all that we love*
*and all that we want: he will be all that we are*
*zealous for, all that we strive for.*
*he will be all that we think about, all our living,*
*all that we talk about, our very breath....As God*
*loves us with a love that is true and pure,*
*a love that never breaks, we too will be joined*
*to him in a never-ending unshakable love,*
*and it will be such a union that our breathing*
*and our thinking and our talking will be 'God'.*
*~ John Cassian*

# Day Ten

**Scripture:** Psalm 27:4-8

**Background:** In the midst of the challenges of life, the Psalmist offers us the secret of his confidence, his delight in communion with God. [Take a few moments to scan through the whole chapter in order to be aware of the context and setting of the text before you begin.]

**The Four Steps of *Lectio Divina*:**

1. *Lectio* (read): [Spend a few moments quieting your heart; then prayerfully acknowledge God's presence.] Read the passage out loud 2-3 times slowly. *What is the word or phrase that stands out to you in this passage?*_____
   _____
   _____

2. *Meditatio* (meditate): Reread the passage slowly in the same or different version. [As you attend to the deeper meaning of the text, pay attention to the feelings and emotions that arise in you. Allow your imagination & senses to be involved as well.] *What did you experience and observe?*_____
   _____
   _____
   _____
   _____
   _____

3. **Oratio** (prayer): Reread the passage one more time. Actively listen and converse with God about the meaning and application of the scripture. [Ask God why this particular word/phrase and emotions is being evoked in you.] *What did you sense God saying and how does he want to respond?*

_____

_____

_____

_____

4. **Contemplatio** (contemplation): A period of silence is kept in order to rest in God. *[End with a prayer of commitment to what you have heard God say. Feel free to speak your prayer or to write it out.]* _____

_____

_____

_____

*[We should] make a private chapel of our heart where we can retire from time to time to commune with God, peacefully, humbly, lovingly...I keep myself in his presence by simple attentiveness and a loving gaze upon God.* ~ Brother Lawrence

*Dear God,*
*Of all the gifts You have given me, perhaps the*
*most precious is Your presence with me. It fills me*
*with joy and awe when I consider that*
*You have chosen my unworthy heart as a dwelling place.*
*Keep me aware of Your nearness.*
~ Terry Glaspey

# Day Eleven

**Scripture:** Psalm 3:3-8

**Background:** David is overwhelmed by his enemies. But his trust in God allows him to take his focus off of his fear and move it to God, his provider. [Take a few moments to scan through the whole chapter in order to be aware of the context and setting of the text before you begin.]

**The Four Steps of *Lectio Divina*:**

1. *Lectio* (read): [Spend a few moments quieting your heart; then prayerfully acknowledge God's presence.] Read the passage out loud 2-3 times slowly. *What is the word or phrase that stands out to you in this passage?*_____

_____

_____

7. *Meditatio* (meditate): Reread the passage slowly in the same or different version. [As you attend to the deeper meaning of the text, pay attention to the feelings and emotions that arise in you. Allow your imagination & senses to be involved as well.] *What did you experience and observe?*_____

_____

_____

_____

_____

_____

8. *Oratio* (prayer): Reread the passage one more time. Actively listen and converse with God about the meaning and application of the scripture. [Ask God why this particular word/phrase and emotions is being evoked in you.] *What did you sense God saying and how does he want to respond?*

_____

_____

_____

_____

_____

9. *Contemplatio* (contemplation): A period of silence is kept in order to rest in God. *[End with a prayer of commitment to what you have heard God say. Feel free to speak your prayer or to write it out.]* _____

_____

_____

_____

*There is no more blessed way of living, than the life of faith based upon a covenant-keeping God - to know that we have no care, for he cares for us; that we need have no fear, except to fear him; that we need have no troubles, because we have cast our burdens upon the Lord, and are conscience that he will sustain us.*
~ Charles Spurgeon

*Fear is born of Satan, and if we would only take time to think a moment we would see that everything Satan says is founded upon a falsehood.*
~ A.B. Simpson

# Day Twelve

**Scripture:** Psalm 37:3-7

**Background:** Since David had often suffered at the hands of ungodly men, he offers us advice on how to react when we become a victim of wicked schemes and malicious tongues. [Take a few moments to scan through the whole chapter in order to be aware of the context and setting of the text before you begin.]

**The Four Steps of *Lectio Divina*:**

1. *Lectio* (read): [Spend a few moments quieting your heart; then prayerfully acknowledge God's presence.] Read the passage out loud 2-3 times slowly. *What is the word or phrase that stands out to you in this passage?*_____

   _____

   _____

2. *Meditatio* (meditate): Reread the passage slowly in the same or different version. [As you attend to the deeper meaning of the text, pay attention to the feelings and emotions that arise in you. Allow your imagination & senses to be involved as well.] *What did you experience and observe?*_____

   _____

   _____

   _____

   _____

42

3. *Oratio* (prayer): Reread the passage one more time. Actively listen and converse with God about the meaning and application of the scripture. [Ask God why this particular word/phrase and emotions is being evoked in you.] *What did you sense God saying and how does he want to respond?*

_____

_____

_____

_____

_____

_____

4. *Contemplatio* (contemplation): A period of silence is kept in order to rest in God. *[End with a prayer of commitment to what you have heard God say. Feel free to speak your prayer or to write it out.]* _____

_____

_____

_____

_____

*A common problem, related to why we may seek to escape silence, is the discovery that it evokes nameless misgivings, guilt feelings, and strange, disquieting anxiety. Anything is better than this mess, and so we flick on the radio or pick up the phone and talk to a friend. If we can pass through these initial fears and remain silent, we may experience a gradual waning of inner chaos. Silence becomes like a creative space in which we regain perspective on the whole.*
~ Susan Annette Muto

# Day Thirteen

**Scripture:** I Kings 19:9-13

**Background:** When Jezebel learns of the defeat and death of the prophets of Baal, she is determined to slay Elijah within a day. God offers provision and rest for Elijah and reminds him of his own self-righteous spirit and that winds, earthquakes and fires cannot accomplish what the gentle whisper of God's love can. [Take a few moments to scan through the whole chapter in order to be aware of the context and setting of the text before you begin.]

## The Four Steps of *Lectio Divina*:

1. *Lectio* (read): [Spend a few moments quieting your heart; then prayerfully acknowledge God's presence.] Read the passage out loud 2-3 times slowly. *What is the word or phrase that stands out to you in this passage?*_____

   _____

   _____

2. *Meditatio* (meditate): Reread the passage slowly in the same or different version. [As you attend to the deeper meaning of the text, pay attention to the feelings and emotions that arise in you. Allow your imagination & senses to be involved as well.] *What did you experience and observe?*_____

   _____

   _____

   _____

3. *Oratio* (prayer): Reread the passage one more time. Actively listen and converse with God about the meaning and application of the scripture. [Ask God why this particular word/phrase and emotions is being evoked in you.] *What did you sense God saying and how does he want to respond?*

_____

_____

_____

_____

4. *Contemplatio* (contemplation): A period of silence is kept in order to rest in God. *[End with a prayer of commitment to what you have heard God say. Feel free to speak your prayer or to write it out.]* _____

_____

_____

_____

*Silence is the very presence of God – always there.*
*But activity hides it. We need to leave activity long*
*enough to discover the Presence – then*
*we can return to activity with it.*
~ Basil Pennington

*Without the practice of silence, these cultural habits*
*(grasping and controlling) will attach themselves to*
*our spiritual disciplines… Silence is bringing ourselves*
*to a point of relinquishing to God our control of our*
*relationship with God… control of our own*
*existence…Silence is the inner act of letting go.*
~ Robert Mulholland

# Day Fourteen

**Scripture:** Colossians 4:2-6

**Background**: Paul is exhorting the Colossians to be diligent in their prayer life. [Take a few moments to scan through the whole chapter in order to be aware of the context and setting of the text before you begin.]

## The Four Steps of *Lectio Divina*:

1. *Lectio* (read): [Spend a few moments quieting your heart; then prayerfully acknowledge God's presence.] Read the passage out loud 2-3 times slowly. *What is the word or phrase that stands out to you in this passage?*_____

_____

_____

2. *Meditatio* (meditate): Reread the passage slowly in the same or different version. [As you attend to the deeper meaning of the text, pay attention to the feelings and emotions that arise in you. Allow your imagination & senses to be involved as well.] *What did you experience and observe?*_____

_____

_____

_____

_____

_____

3. *Oratio* (prayer): Reread the passage one more time. Actively listen and converse with God about the meaning and application of the scripture. [Ask God why this particular word/phrase and emotions is being evoked in you.] *What did you sense God saying and how does he want to respond?*

_____

_____

_____

_____

4. *Contemplatio* (contemplation): A period of silence is kept in order to rest in God. *[End with a prayer of commitment to what you have heard God say. Feel free to speak your prayer or to write it out.]* _____

_____

_____

*How much prayer meant to Jesus! It was not only his*
*regular habit, but his resort in every emergency...*
*When perplexed he prayed...When hungry for fellowship*
*he found it in prayer...If tempted, he prayed. If criticized,*
*he prayed. If fatigued in body or wearied in spirit,*
*he had recourse to his one unfailing habit of prayer.*
*Prayer brought him unmeasured power at the beginning,*
*and kept the flow unbroken and undiminished. There*
*was no emergency, no difficulty, no necessity, no*
*temptation that would not yield to prayer...Shall not*
*we, who have been tracing these steps in his prayer-life,*
*go back over them again and again until*
*we breathe in his very spirit of prayer?*
*~ S.D. Gordon*

# Day Fifteen

**Scripture:** Psalm 103:1-5

**Background:** The 103rd Psalm speaks with a majestic beat of thanksgiving, which can mirror our own deepest emotions. [Take a few moments to scan through the whole chapter in order to be aware of the context and setting of the text before you begin.]

**The Four Steps of *Lectio Divina*:**

1. *Lectio* (read): [Spend a few moments quieting your heart; then prayerfully acknowledge God's presence.] Read the passage out loud 2-3 times slowly. *What is the word or phrase that stands out to you in this passage?*_____

   _____

   _____

2. *Meditatio* (meditate): Reread the passage slowly in the same or different version. [As you attend to the deeper meaning of the text, pay attention to the feelings and emotions that arise in you. Allow your imagination & senses to be involved as well.] *What did you experience and observe?*_____

   _____

   _____

   _____

   _____

   _____

3. *Oratio* (prayer): Reread the passage one more time. Actively listen and converse with God about the meaning and application of the scripture. [Ask God why this particular word/phrase and emotions is being evoked in you.] *What did you sense God saying and how does he want to respond?*

_____

_____

_____

_____

_____


4. *Contemplatio* (contemplation): A period of silence is kept in order to rest in God. *[End with a prayer of commitment to what you have heard God say. Feel free to speak your prayer or to write it out.]* _____

_____

_____

_____


*The Psalmists in telling everyone to praise God are doing what all men do when they speak of what they care about.*
~ C.S. Lewis

*Prayer and praise are the oars by which a man may row his boat into the deep waters of the knowledge of Christ.*
~ Charles Spurgeon

*Worship is our innermost being responding with praise for all that God is, through our attitudes, actions, thoughts, and words, based on the truth of God as he has revealed himself.*
~ John MacArthur

# Day Sixteen

**Scripture:** Ephesians 3:14-19

**Background**: Paul prays this prayer as he thinks about what these Gentiles had been by nature and what they have become through a relationship with Christ. [Take a few moments to scan through the whole chapter in order to be aware of the context and setting of the text before you begin.]

**The Four Steps of** *Lectio Divina*:

1. *Lectio* (read): [Spend a few moments quieting your heart; then prayerfully acknowledge God's presence.] Read the passage out loud 2-3 times slowly. *What is the word or phrase that stands out to you in this passage?*_____

   _____

   _____

2. *Meditatio* (meditate): Reread the passage slowly in the same or different version. [As you attend to the deeper meaning of the text, pay attention to the feelings and emotions that arise in you. Allow your imagination & senses to be involved as well.] *What did you experience and observe?*_____

   _____

   _____

   _____

   _____

   _____

3. *Oratio* (prayer): Reread the passage one more time. Actively listen and converse with God about the meaning and application of the scripture. [Ask God why this particular word/phrase and emotions is being evoked in you.] *What did you sense God saying and how does he want to respond?*

_____

_____

_____

_____

4. *Contemplatio* (contemplation): A period of silence is kept in order to rest in God. *[End with a prayer of commitment to what you have heard God say. Feel free to speak your prayer or to write it out.]* _____

_____

_____

_____

*We should be astonished at the goodness of God, stunned that he should bother to call us by name, our mouths wide open at his love, bewildered that at this very moment we are standing on holy ground.*
~ Brennan Manning

*There is no pit so deep, that God's love is not deeper still.*
~ Corrie ten Boom

*A refusal to believe that God loves us is the unbelief which destroys the soul.*
~ Edward Norris Kirk

# Day Seventeen

**Scripture:** I Peter 5:5-11

**Background**: This final chapter of I Peter contains exhortations to the believers. In verses five through eleven, Peter focuses on humility, shown in relation to others and to God. [Take a few moments to scan through the whole chapter in order to be aware of the context and setting of the text before you begin.]

**The Four Steps of *Lectio Divina*:**

1.  *Lectio* (read): [Spend a few moments quieting your heart; then prayerfully acknowledge God's presence.] Read the passage out loud 2-3 times slowly. *What is the word or phrase that stands out to you in this passage?*_____

    _____

    _____

2.  *Meditatio* (meditate): Reread the passage slowly in the same or different version. [As you attend to the deeper meaning of the text, pay attention to the feelings and emotions that arise in you. Allow your imagination & senses to be involved as well.] *What did you experience and observe?*_____

    _____

    _____

    _____

    _____

    _____

3. *Oratio* (prayer): Reread the passage one more time. Actively listen and converse with God about the meaning and application of the scripture. [Ask God why this particular word/phrase and emotions is being evoked in you.] *What did you sense God saying and how does he want to respond?*

_____

_____

_____

_____

4. *Contemplatio* (contemplation): A period of silence is kept in order to rest in God. *[End with a prayer of commitment to what you have heard God say. Feel free to speak your prayer or to write it out.]* _____

_____

_____

_____

*The greatest test of whether the holiness we profess to seek or to attain is truth and life will be whether it produces an increasing humility in us. The chief mark of counterfeit holiness is lack of humility. The holiest will be the humblest.*
~ Andrew Murray

*The cross is the greatest example of humility and devotion in the universe. Jesus put your needs ahead of his own. He considered you more valuable than himself.*
~ Chip Ingram

*Humility is to make a right estimate of one's self.*
~ Charles Spurgeon

# Day Eighteen

**Scripture:** Psalm 40:1-3

**Background:** Even though Psalm 40 can be applied to Jesus' resurrection and agony on the cross, we find it applicable to our own lives as well. [Take a few moments to scan through the whole chapter in order to be aware of the context and setting of the text before you begin.]

**The Four Steps of** *Lectio Divina*:

1. *Lectio* (read): [Spend a few moments quieting your heart; then prayerfully acknowledge God's presence.] Read the passage out loud 2-3 times slowly. *What is the word or phrase that stands out to you in this passage?*_____

_____

_____

2. *Meditatio* (meditate): Reread the passage slowly in the same or different version. [As you attend to the deeper meaning of the text, pay attention to the feelings and emotions that arise in you. Allow your imagination & senses to be involved as well.] *What did you experience and observe?*_____

_____

_____

_____

_____

_____

54

3. *Oratio* (prayer): Reread the passage one more time. Actively listen and converse with God about the meaning and application of the scripture. [Ask God why this particular word/phrase and emotions is being evoked in you.] *What did you sense God saying and how does he want to respond?*

_____

_____

_____

_____

_____

_____

4. *Contemplatio* (contemplation): A period of silence is kept in order to rest in God. *[End with a prayer of commitment to what you have heard God say. Feel free to speak your prayer or to write it out.]* _____

_____

_____

_____

_____

*If the Lord Jehovah makes us wait,*
*let us do so with our whole hearts;*
*for blessed are all they that wait for him.*
*he is worth waiting for.*
*The waiting itself is beneficial to us: it tries faith,*
*exercises patience, trains submission,*
*and endears the blessing when it comes.*
*The Lord's people have always been a waiting people.*
~ Charles Spurgeon

# Day Nineteen

**Scripture:** Ephesians 4:29-5:2

**Background:** In Ephesians 4:17-5:21 Paul begins an appeal for a new morality. He urges Christians to put off every trace of their past life and to put on the virtues of Christ. [Take a few moments to scan through the whole chapter in order to be aware of the context and setting of the text before you begin.]

**The Four Steps of *Lectio Divina*:**

1. *Lectio* (read): [Spend a few moments quieting your heart; then prayerfully acknowledge God's presence.] Read the passage out loud 2-3 times slowly. *What is the word or phrase that stands out to you in this passage?*_____

   _____

   _____

2. *Meditatio* (meditate): Reread the passage slowly in the same or different version. [As you attend to the deeper meaning of the text, pay attention to the feelings and emotions that arise in you. Allow your imagination & senses to be involved as well.] *What did you experience and observe?*_____

   _____

   _____

   _____

   _____

   _____

3. *Oratio* (prayer): Reread the passage one more time. Actively listen and converse with God about the meaning and application of the scripture. [Ask God why this particular word/phrase and emotions is being evoked in you.] *What did you sense God saying and how does he want to respond?*

_____

_____

_____

_____

_____

4. *Contemplatio* (contemplation): A period of silence is kept in order to rest in God. [*End with a prayer of commitment to what you have heard God say. Feel free to speak your prayer or to write it out.*] _____

_____

_____

_____

*Christ's command is that we should love one another as he loves us; to give his life was his way of loving. (Luke 6:31)*
~ Anthony of Sourozh

*The proof that you love someone is not that you have warm affectionate feelings toward them. The proof is in your actions, your words and your sacrifice, your willingness to give the best of yourself and your willingness to get nothing in return.*
~ Katherine Walden

*The desire of love is to give. The desire of lust is to get.*
~ Ed Cole

# Day Twenty

**Scripture:** Psalm 119:9-16

**Background:** Psalm 119 is divided into twenty-two sections, one for each letter of the Hebrew alphabet. This section, verses 9-16 deals with the importance of God's Word. [Take a few moments to scan through the whole chapter in order to be aware of the context and setting of the text before you begin.]

**The Four Steps of *Lectio Divina*:**

1.  *Lectio* (read): [Spend a few moments quieting your heart; then prayerfully acknowledge God's presence.] Read the passage out loud 2-3 times slowly. *What is the word or phrase that stands out to you in this passage?*_____

    _____

    _____

2.  *Meditatio* (meditate): Reread the passage slowly in the same or different version. [As you attend to the deeper meaning of the text, pay attention to the feelings and emotions that arise in you. Allow your imagination & senses to be involved as well.] *What did you experience and observe?*_____

    _____

    _____

    _____

    _____

3. *Oratio* (prayer): Reread the passage one more time. Actively listen and converse with God about the meaning and application of the scripture. [Ask God why this particular word/phrase and emotions is being evoked in you.] *What did you sense God saying and how does he want to respond?*

_____

_____

_____

_____

4. *Contemplatio* (contemplation): A period of silence is kept in order to rest in God. *[End with a prayer of commitment to what you have heard God say. Feel free to speak your prayer or to write it out.]* _____

_____

_____

*God's Word must be so strongly fixed in our minds that it becomes the dominant influence in our thoughts, our attitudes, and our actions. One of the most effective ways of influencing our minds is through memorizing Scripture.*
~ Jerry Bridges

*As you spend time in God's Word and understand his love, the Holy Spirit will create new desires within you to love and serve others like never before.*
~ Chip Ingram

*God's Word will never fall into disrepair. But here's what happens when we don't travel on it: We fall into disrepair!*
~ David Jeremiah

# Day Twenty-One

**Scripture:** Psalm 62:5-8

**Background**: The message of Psalm 62 is that God is the only true refuge. This Psalm may have been inspired by Absalom's rebellion. [Take a few moments to scan through the whole chapter in order to be aware of the context and setting of the text before you begin.]

**The Four Steps of *Lectio Divina*:**

1. *Lectio* (read): [Spend a few moments quieting your heart; then prayerfully acknowledge God's presence.] Read the passage out loud 2-3 times slowly. *What is the word or phrase that stands out to you in this passage?*_____

   _____

   _____

2. *Meditatio* (meditate): Reread the passage slowly in the same or different version. [As you attend to the deeper meaning of the text, pay attention to the feelings and emotions that arise in you. Allow your imagination & senses to be involved as well.] *What did you experience and observe?*_____

   _____

   _____

   _____

   _____

   _____

3. *Oratio* (prayer): Reread the passage one more time. Actively listen and converse with God about the meaning and application of the scripture. [Ask God why this particular word/phrase and emotions is being evoked in you.] *What did you sense God saying and how does he want to respond?*

_____

_____

_____

_____

4. *Contemplatio* (contemplation): A period of silence is kept in order to rest in God. *[End with a prayer of commitment to what you have heard God say. Feel free to speak your prayer or to write it out.]* _____

_____

_____

*Do not look to your hope, but to Christ,*
*the source of your hope.*
~ Charles Spurgeon

*Many things are possible for the person who has hope.*
*Even more is possible for the person who has faith.*
*And still more is possible for the person who knows*
*how to love. But everything is possible for the*
*person who practices all three virtues.*
~ Brother Lawrence

*The presence of hope in the invincible*
*sovereignty of God drives out fear.*
~ John Piper

# Day Twenty-Two

**Scripture:** Galatians 2:19-21

**Background**: Paul declares that the believer's rule of life is Christ, not the law. We are identified with Christ in his death. [Take a few moments to scan through the whole chapter in order to be aware of the context and setting of the text before you begin.]

**The Four Steps of *Lectio Divina*:**

1. *Lectio* (read): [Spend a few moments quieting your heart; then prayerfully acknowledge God's presence.] Read the passage out loud 2-3 times slowly. *What is the word or phrase that stands out to you in this passage?*_____

_____

_____

5. *Meditatio* (meditate): Reread the passage slowly in the same or different version. [As you attend to the deeper meaning of the text, pay attention to the feelings and emotions that arise in you. Allow your imagination & senses to be involved as well.] *What did you experience and observe?*_____

_____

_____

_____

_____

_____

6. *Oratio* (prayer): Reread the passage one more time. Actively listen and converse with God about the meaning and application of the scripture. [Ask God why this particular word/phrase and emotions is being evoked in you.] *What did you sense God saying and how does he want to respond?*

_____

_____

_____

_____

_____

_____

7. *Contemplatio* (contemplation): A period of silence is kept in order to rest in God. *[End with a prayer of commitment to what you have heard God say. Feel free to speak your prayer or to write it out.]* _____

_____

_____

_____

*There are plenty to follow our Lord half-way, but not the other half. They will give up possessions, friends and honors, but it touches them too closely to disown themselves. It is just this astonishing life which is willing to follow him the other half, sincerely to disown itself, this life which intends complete obedience, without any reservations, that I would propose to you in all humility, in all boldness, in all seriousness. I mean this literally, utterly, completely.... commit your lives in unreserved obedience to him.*
~ Thomas R. Kelly

# Day Twenty-Three

**Scripture:** Colossians 3:12-17

**Background:** In Colossians 3 Paul is giving them some rules for Holy Living. [Take a few moments to scan through the whole chapter in order to be aware of the context and setting of the text before you begin.]

## The Four Steps of *Lectio Divina:*

1. *Lectio* (read): [Spend a few moments quieting your heart; then prayerfully acknowledge God's presence.] Read the passage out loud 2-3 times slowly. *What is the word or phrase that stands out to you in this passage?*_____

   _____

   _____

2. *Meditatio* (meditate): Reread the passage slowly in the same or different version. [As you attend to the deeper meaning of the text, pay attention to the feelings and emotions that arise in you. Allow your imagination & senses to be involved as well.] *What did you experience and observe?*_____

   _____

   _____

   _____

   _____

   _____

3. *Oratio* (prayer): Reread the passage one more time. Actively listen and converse with God about the meaning and application of the scripture. [Ask God why this particular word/phrase and emotions is being evoked in you.] *What did you sense God saying and how does he want to respond?*

_____

_____

_____

_____

_____

4. *Contemplatio* (contemplation): A period of silence is kept in order to rest in God. *[End with a prayer of commitment to what you have heard God say. Feel free to speak your prayer or to write it out.]* _____

_____

_____

_____

*There is no neutrality between gratitude and ingratitude. Those who are not grateful soon begin to complain of everything. Gratitude, though, is more than a mental exercise, more than a formula of words....To be grateful is to recognize the Love of God in everything he has given us....Gratitude therefore takes nothing for granted, is never unresponsive, is constantly awakening to new wonder and to praise of the goodness of God. For the grateful man knows that God is good, not by hearsay but by experience. And that is what makes all the difference.*
~ Thomas Merton

# Day Twenty-Four

**Scripture:** Psalm 73:21-28

**Background:** Asaph is speaking about God's goodness to Israel. Despite their ignorant behavior, God has not forsaken them. He recites God's faithfulness and goodness. [Take a few moments to scan through the whole chapter in order to be aware of the context and setting of the text before you begin.]

**The Four Steps of *Lectio Divina*:**

1. *Lectio* (read): [Spend a few moments quieting your heart; then prayerfully acknowledge God's presence.] Read the passage out loud 2-3 times slowly. *What is the word or phrase that stands out to you in this passage?*_____
   _____
   _____

2. *Meditatio* (meditate): Reread the passage slowly in the same or different version. [As you attend to the deeper meaning of the text, pay attention to the feelings and emotions that arise in you. Allow your imagination & senses to be involved as well.] *What did you experience and observe?*_____
   _____
   _____
   _____
   _____

3. *Oratio* (prayer): Reread the passage one more time. Actively listen and converse with God about the meaning and application of the scripture. [Ask God why this particular word/phrase and emotions is being evoked in you.] *What did you sense God saying and how does he want to respond?*

_____

_____

_____

_____

4. *Contemplatio* (contemplation): A period of silence is kept in order to rest in God. *[End with a prayer of commitment to what you have heard God say. Feel free to speak your prayer or to write it out.]* _____

_____

_____

*May God so fill us today with the heart of Christ*
*that we may glow with the divine fire of holy desire.*
~ A.B. Simpson

*The stiff and wooden quality about our religious*
*lives is a result of our lack of holy desire.*
*Complacency is a deadly foe of all spiritual growth.*
*Acute desire must be present or there*
*will be no manifestation of Christ to his people.*
~ A.W. Tozer

*The reason we are not able to see God is the*
*faintness of our desire.*
~ Meister Eckhart

## Day Twenty-Five

**Scripture:** Psalm 125:1-5

**Background**: In this scripture Mt. Zion signifies the ultimate in stability and strength. The Psalmist is likening this to the man of faith who has built his life on the solid rock. [Take a few moments to scan through the whole chapter in order to be aware of the context and setting of the text before you begin.]

**The Four Steps of *Lectio Divina*:**

1. *Lectio* (read): [Spend a few moments quieting your heart; then prayerfully acknowledge God's presence.] Read the passage out loud 2-3 times slowly. *What is the word or phrase that stands out to you in this passage?*_____

    _____

    _____

2. *Meditatio* (meditate): Reread the passage slowly in the same or different version. [As you attend to the deeper meaning of the text, pay attention to the feelings and emotions that arise in you. Allow your imagination & senses to be involved as well.] *What did you experience and observe?*_____

    _____

    _____

    _____

    _____

    _____

3. *Oratio* (prayer): Reread the passage one more time. Actively listen and converse with God about the meaning and application of the scripture. [Ask God why this particular word/phrase and emotions is being evoked in you.] *What did you sense God saying and how does he want to respond?*

_____

_____

_____

_____

4. *Contemplatio* (contemplation): A period of silence is kept in order to rest in God. *[End with a prayer of commitment to what you have heard God say. Feel free to speak your prayer or to write it out.]* _____

_____

_____

*Remember the goodness of God in the frost of adversity.*
~ Charles Spurgeon

*Receive every day as a resurrection from death, as*
*a new enjoyment of life; meet every rising sun with*
*such sentiments of God's goodness, as if you had seen it,*
*and all things, new-created upon your account: and*
*under the sense of so great a blessing, let your joyful*
*heart praise and magnify so good and glorious a Creator.*
~ William Law

*Prayer is the way and means God has appointed for the*
*communication of the blessings of his goodness to his people.*
~ A.W. Pink

# Day Twenty-Six

**Scripture:** Lamentations 3:19-32

**Background**: The prophet (probably Jeremiah) was remembering his bitter plight and Israel's captivity. Yet he transfers his eyes off himself and on to the Lord, which revives his hope. [Take a few moments to scan through the whole chapter in order to be aware of the context and setting of the text before you begin.]

**The Four Steps of *Lectio Divina*:**

1. *Lectio* (read): [Spend a few moments quieting your heart; then prayerfully acknowledge God's presence.] Read the passage out loud 2-3 times slowly. *What is the word or phrase that stands out to you in this passage?*_____

   _____

   _____

2. *Meditatio* (meditate): Reread the passage slowly in the same or different version. [As you attend to the deeper meaning of the text, pay attention to the feelings and emotions that arise in you. Allow your imagination & senses to be involved as well.] *What did you experience and observe?*_____

   _____

   _____

   _____

   _____

3. *Oratio* (prayer): Reread the passage one more time. Actively listen and converse with God about the meaning and application of the scripture. [Ask God why this particular word/phrase and emotions is being evoked in you.] *What did you sense God saying and how does he want to respond?*

_____

_____

_____

_____

_____


4. *Contemplatio* (contemplation): A period of silence is kept in order to rest in God. *[End with a prayer of commitment to what you have heard God say. Feel free to speak your prayer or to write it out.]* _____

_____

_____

_____


*Remember that even Jesus' most scathing denunciation - a blistering diatribe against the religious leaders of Jerusalem in Matthew 23 - ends with Christ weeping over Jerusalem. Compassion colored everything he did.*
~ John MacArthur

*We may think that severity (as God leads his children) is inconsistent with what we know of God's gentleness and compassion. But that is because we do not appreciate how seriously God loves us, and how determined he is that we should have his best, even if it means pain.*
~ Sinclair B. Ferguson

# Day Twenty-Seven

**Scripture:** II Corinthians 4:16-18

**Background:** Paul did not lose heart through all the suffering and afflictions he endured. In this chapter he is encouraging us not to lose heart either. [Take a few moments to scan through the whole chapter in order to be aware of the context and setting of the text before you begin.]

**The Four Steps of *Lectio Divina*:**

1. *Lectio* (read): [Spend a few moments quieting your heart; then prayerfully acknowledge God's presence.] Read the passage out loud 2-3 times slowly. *What is the word or phrase that stands out to you in this passage?*_____

   _____

   _____

2. *Meditatio* (meditate): Reread the passage slowly in the same or different version. [As you attend to the deeper meaning of the text, pay attention to the feelings and emotions that arise in you. Allow your imagination & senses to be involved as well.] *What did you experience and observe?*_____

   _____

   _____

   _____

   _____

   _____

3. *Oratio* (prayer): Reread the passage one more time. Actively listen and converse with God about the meaning and application of the scripture. [Ask God why this particular word/phrase and emotions is being evoked in you.] *What did you sense God saying and how does he want to respond?*

_____

_____

_____

_____

_____

4. *Contemplatio* (contemplation): A period of silence is kept in order to rest in God. *[End with a prayer of commitment to what you have heard God say. Feel free to speak your prayer or to write it out.]* _____

_____

_____

_____

_____

*Difficulties and obstacles are God's challenges to faith.*
*When hindrances confront us in the path of duty,*
*we are to recognize them as vessels for faith to*
*fill with the fullness and all-sufficiency of Jesus.*
~ A.B. Simpson

*God will not permit any troubles to come upon us,*
*unless he has a specific plan by which great blessing*
*can comeout of the difficulty.*
~ Peter Marshall

# Day Twenty-Eight

**Scripture:** Jeremiah 17:5-8

**Background**: Judah's idolatry and lack of trust in God will result in her being sent off into captivity. The prophet reminds us of the difference between trusting in God and trusting in man. [Take a few moments to scan through the whole chapter in order to be aware of the context and setting of the text before you begin.]

**The Four Steps of *Lectio Divina*:**

1. *Lectio* (read): [Spend a few moments quieting your heart; then prayerfully acknowledge God's presence.] Read the passage out loud 2-3 times slowly. *What is the word or phrase that stands out to you in this passage?*_____

   _____

   _____

2. *Meditatio* (meditate): Reread the passage slowly in the same or different version. [As you attend to the deeper meaning of the text, pay attention to the feelings and emotions that arise in you. Allow your imagination & senses to be involved as well.] *What did you experience and observe?*_____

   _____

   _____

   _____

   _____

   _____

3.  *Oratio* (prayer): Reread the passage one more time. Actively listen and converse with God about the meaning and application of the scripture. [Ask God why this particular word/phrase and emotions is being evoked in you.] *What did you sense God saying and how does he want to respond?*

    _____

    _____

    _____

    _____

    _____


4.  *Contemplatio* (contemplation): A period of silence is kept in order to rest in God. *[End with a prayer of commitment to what you have heard God say. Feel free to speak your prayer or to write it out.]* _____

    _____

    _____

> *Walk with God in holy trust, responding*
> *to his initiatives rather than trying to*
> *make things fit your plans.*
> ~ Sarah Young

> *Worry, by nature, is the product of a lack of*
> *faith and trust in God.*
> ~ John MacArthur

> *Trust the past to God's mercy, the present to*
> *God's love, and the future to God's providence.*
> ~ St. Augustine

# Day Twenty-Nine

**Scripture:** Deuteronomy 30:14-20

**Background**: Moses is concerned that the people of Israel will break the covenant they made with God just prior to their entrance into the Promise Land. He gives them a clear choice in regard to following God's commands: choose life (obedience) or death (disobedience). [Take a few moments to scan through the whole chapter in order to be aware of the context and setting of the text before you begin.]

**The Four Steps of *Lectio Divina*:**

1. *Lectio* (read): [Spend a few moments quieting your heart; then prayerfully acknowledge God's presence.] Read the passage out loud 2-3 times slowly. *What is the word or phrase that stands out to you in this passage?*_____

_____

_____

2. *Meditatio* (meditate): Reread the passage slowly in the same or different version. [As you attend to the deeper meaning of the text, pay attention to the feelings and emotions that arise in you. Allow your imagination & senses to be involved as well.] *What did you experience and observe?*_____

_____

_____

_____

_____

3. *Oratio* (prayer): Reread the passage one more time. Actively listen and converse with God about the meaning and application of the scripture. [Ask God why this particular word/phrase and emotions is being evoked in you.] *What did you sense God saying and how does he want to respond?*

_____

_____

_____

4. *Contemplatio* (contemplation): A period of silence is kept in order to rest in God. *[End with a prayer of commitment to what you have heard God say. Feel free to speak your prayer or to write it out.]* _____

_____

_____

_____

*Choosing life seems like the reasonable thing to do...*
*It remains a mystery to me that we often find*
*ourselves choosing what diminishes life and leaves*
*us less than we were before....Jesus always invites*
*us to choose life by forsaking our way of life for*
*his way of life...(But) choosing to walk with Jesus*
*in a culture that ridicules faithfulness and glorifies*
*violence is to choose a way with cost attached.*
*At times it may seem that the cost of choosing*
*life is too high, but when you stop and think about it,*
*choosing life is the only reasonable choice to make.*
*~ Rueben P. Job*

# Day Thirty

**Scripture:** Matthew 6:25-34

**Background:** The Sermon on the Mount (Matthew 5-7) is Jesus' longest portion of teaching. It contains the central tenets of Christian discipleship, reminding us to trust God and seek him instead of worrying. [Take a few moments to scan through the whole chapter in order to be aware of the context and setting of the text before you begin.]

**The Four Steps of *Lectio Divina*:**

1. *Lectio* (read): [Spend a few moments quieting your heart; then prayerfully acknowledge God's presence.] Read the passage out loud 2-3 times slowly. *What is the word or phrase that stands out to you in this passage?* _____
   _____
   _____

2. *Meditatio* (meditate): Reread the passage slowly in the same or different version. [As you attend to the deeper meaning of the text, pay attention to the feelings and emotions that arise in you. Allow your imagination & senses to be involved as well.] *What did you experience and observe?* _____
   _____
   _____
   _____
   _____
   _____

3. *Oratio* (prayer): Reread the passage one more time. Actively listen and converse with God about the meaning and application of the scripture. [Ask God why this particular word/phrase and emotions is being evoked in you.] *What did you sense God saying and how does he want to respond?*

_____

_____

_____

_____

4. *Contemplatio* (contemplation): A period of silence is kept in order to rest in God. *[End with a prayer of commitment to what you have heard God say. Feel free to speak your prayer or to write it out.]* _____

_____

_____

*Sooner or later you will have to put God first in your life, that is to say, your own true spiritual development must become the only thing that really matters. It need not...be the only thing in your life, but it must be the first thing. When this happens you will find that you have got rid of a great deal of the unnecessary junk that most people carry about; mental junk, of course, although physical junk is very apt to follow upon this. You will find that you will do a great deal less running about after things that do not matter and only waste your time and energy, when once you have put God first. Your life will become simpler and quieter, but in the true sense, richer and infinitely more worthwhile.*
~ Emmet Fox

# CHAPTER 4

## MORE SCRIPTURES FOR PRACTICING *LECTIO DIVINA*

Now that you have finished the 30 days of *Lectio Divina*, you have become aware that it is the Spirit that is the director of this process. Every time you practice *Lectio Divina* you will find it to be unique and revitalizing as the Spirit leads the process.

You will never use up your resources in practicing *Lectio Divina* because God's Word is inexhaustible. I have found it useful, at times, to even revisit passages of scripture since God's Word is always speaking something fresh and new to us through his Spirit!

I hope you will use the additional scriptures listed below in both charts as you continue practicing *Lectio Divina*. Or you may want to choose your own scriptures as you continue this journey in intimacy with the Father. I have listed the steps again to refer to as you continue practicing *Lectio Divina*. Use a journal to record your responses, so that you can remember what God is saying to you each day.

I especially encourage you to use *Lectio Divina* with the Qualities of God (in this chapter). It will refresh your View of God and offer you opportunities for delighting in Who he is. In the Qualities of God chart, I have given you the scripture verse where you can find the quality of God, and then a longer passage in which to practice your *Lectio Divina*.

God bless you as you continue meeting with God each day through this wonderful practice of *Lectio Divina*!

# The Four Steps of *Lectio Divina*

1. *Lectio Divina* (read): [Spend a few moments quieting your heart; then prayerfully acknowledge God's presence.] Read the passage out loud 2-3 times slowly. *What is the word or phrase that stands out to you in this passage?*_____

   _____

2. *Meditatio* (meditate): Reread the passage slowly (same or different version). [As you attend to the deeper meaning of the text, pay attention to the feelings and emotions that arise in you. Allow your imagination & senses to be involved as well.] *What did you experience and observe?*_____

   _____

3. *Oratio* (prayer): Reread the passage one more time. Actively listen and converse with God about the meaning and application of the scripture. [Ask God why this particular word/phrase and emotions is being evoked in you.] *What did you sense God saying and how does he want you to respond?*_____

   _____

4. *Contemplatio* (contemplation): A period of silence is kept in order to rest in God. *[End with a prayer of commitment to what you have heard God say. Feel free to speak your prayer or to write it out.]*_____

   _____

# Additional Scriptures for *Lectio Divina*

| Old Testament | New Testament |
|---|---|
| Genesis 50:15-21 | Matthew 11:28-29 |
| Exodus 3:1-6 | Mark 10:35-45 |
| Exodus 14:10-14 | Luke 19: 1-10 |
| Numbers 6:22-27 | John 14:1-5 |
| Psalm 18:1-3 | John 14:23-27 |
| Psalm 20:1-5 | John 15:1-5 |
| Psalm 23:1-3 | Romans 8:31-39 |
| Psalm 34:1-8 | Romans 12:1-2 |
| Psalm 85:8-13 | I Cor. 13:3-8 |
| Psalm 91:1-8 | II Cor. 1:3-5 |
| Psalm 121:1-8 | II Cor. 2:14-17 |
| Psalm 139:13-18 | II Cor. 4:7-12 |
| Psalm 143:8-10 | II Cor. 10:3-6 |
| Proverbs 3:1-8 | II Cor. 12:8-10 |
| Isaiah 30:15-18 | Galatians 5:16-26 |
| Isaiah 30:18-21 | Ephesians 1:15-23 |
| Isaiah 32:16-20 | Ephesians 2:13-16 |
| Isaiah 40:28-31 | Ephesians 6:10-18 |
| Isaiah 41:9-10 | Philippians 2:5-11 |
| Isaiah 42:5-9 | Philippians 3:7-14 |
| Isaiah 43:18-21 | Philippians 4:10-13 |
| Isaiah 49:13-16 | Colossians 2:6-10 |
| Isaiah 50:9-11 | I Thess. 5:16-24 |
| Isaiah 54:5-10 | Hebrews 4:12-16 |
| Isaiah 55:6-12 | Hebrews 12:1-3 |
| Isaiah 58:11-12 | James 1:2-8 |
| Isaiah 64:8-9 | James 1:22-27 |
| Jeremiah 6:19 | James 3:1-12 |
| Zephaniah 3:14-17 | James 4:7-10 |
| Habakkuk 3:17-19 | I Peter 5:5-11 |

# Qualities of God

| Characteristic | Meaning | Scripture |
| --- | --- | --- |
| Immutable | God never differs from himself; he changes not | Mal. 3:6 (Mal. 3:6-7) |
| Infinite | God is Limitless; his being knows no limit | Ps. 147:5 (Ps. 147:2-5) |
| Everlasting | No beginning, no end; God's time is different | Ps. 90:2 (Ps. 90:1-2) |
| Omniscient | He possesses perfect knowledge | I Sam. 2:3, NKJ (I Sam. 2:1-3) |
| Omnipotent | He has all power, limitless | Rev. 19:6, NKJ (Rev. 19:4-6) |
| Omnipresent | God is everywhere present; always near us | Ps. 119:151 (Ps. 119:148-152) |
| Transcendent | God is exalted far above the created universe | Ps. 57:5 (Ps. 57:2-5) |

| | | |
|---|---|---|
| Merciful | Actively compassionate | Dan. 9:9 (Dan. 9:7-10) |
| Gracious | God of grace; goodness of God | II Chron. 30:6-9 |
| Love | Takes pleasure in; enjoys; intimate; Unconditional | Ps. 36:7 (Ps. 36:5-10) |
| Holy | Infinite; Incomprehensible; fullness of purity | Isa. 6:3 (Isa. 6:1-4) |
| Sovereign | Ruler; is Supreme, the Highest | Isa. 40:10 (Isa. 40:9-11) |
| Good | Kind; benevolent; bestows blessings; shows love and kindness | Ps.27:13 (Ps. 27:7-14) |
| Faithful | God is faithful & will always do what he says | Lam. 3:23 (Lam. 3:22-26) |

# Conclusion

I have provided some additional resources for you as you journey with Christ using *Lectio Divina*. Appendix A will give you some ideas for **Quieting your heart** as you begin *Lectio Divina*. Appendix B will give you some ideas on how to **Enhance your Relationship with God** by clearing out any debris in your life. Appendix C offers you a list of some **Additional Spiritual Formation Exercises** that can help engage both the mind & heart.

Do not be concerned if at first *Lectio Divina* feels a bit foreign to you. It is not easy to learn how to hear God's voice and to form an intimacy with him just by reading a book. However, you can experience it by doing it! God will be present if you show up, calm your heart, and listen!

The Bible will be your main resource for material for your time in *Lectio Divina*. But you may also want to consider doing a form of *Lectio Divina* as you read some of the classic writings of Christian writers of the past who were inspired by God. Pondering on what they have written, using the steps of *Lectio Divina*, will bring deeper meaning to their words.

A good start would be to purchase one of these classics by Renovare, *Spiritual Classics* and *Devotional Classics*. These selected readings contain many of the great spiritual writers of the past, such as Augustine of Hippo, Blaise Pascal, Francis of Assisi, Dietrich Bonhoeffer, Julian of Norwich, Martin Luther, Søren Kierkegaard, Teresa of

Ávila, Thomas Merton, John Calvin, Frederick Buechner, Evelyn Underhill, A.W. Tozer, G.K. Chesterton, Thomas More, Amy Carmichael, Brother Lawrence, Madame Guyon, Hannah Whitall Smith, Ignatius of Loyola, Jean-Pierre de Caussade, C.S. Lewis, Henri Nouwen, Thomas à Kempis, and many more.

May you be blessed as you hunger and thirst after a deeper relationship with God. May you sense the smile of God on you as you spend time focusing on him. May you hear his voice each and every day as you listen to him.

In closing, may the words of this Psalm be your unceasing prayer as you experience intimate moments with the Father.

*"Let the words of my mouth and*
*the meditation of my heart*
*be acceptable in your sight,*
*O Lord, my strength and my Redeemer."*
(Ps. 19:14, NKJ).

# Appendix A

## Helpful Guidelines for
## Quieting your Heart

A. Ways to Connect with God

1. Sit in his presence adoring him and delighting in him (Ps. 37:4), and expressing your love to him

2. Magnify the Lord. Magnify means to make larger. John the Baptist said, "he must increase, but I must decrease" (Jn. 3:30, NKJ). In other words, he must become more important while I become less important. This happens as we focus on God by glorifying him, praising him, and placing our thoughts and mind on him.

3. Give thanks. The scriptures remind us that we can enter his presence with thanksgiving (Ps. 100:4) and gratitude. Pastor Robin Ricks (Bellefontaine, OH) says, "If the enemy comes to the battle armed with facts about your past, and fears, doubts, and lies....and the believer comes to the same war zone armed with a thankful heart, the believer wins the battle every time". Thankfulness can help destroy the distractions of the enemy!

4. Worship him. Psalm 100:2 reminds us to "Worship the Lord with gladness. Come before him, singing with joy." You can sing along with a worship tape or simply listen to a worship song, which will help you sense God's presence.

B. Palms Down, Palms Up[34]
- This can help when you may feel distracted by things that might have previously happened in your day or from things on your mind.
- Place your palms down (in the air or on your lap) as a symbolic indication of your desire to release what is on your mind (weakness, problem, distraction)
- Name what it is as you symbolically give it to Jesus, by dropping your hands]
- Turn your palms up to demonstrate your openness to receive what God has for you - his presence, his love, or something he wants to say

C. The Use of Breath and Breathing Practices
   1. Proper Breathing:
- Slowly breathe in through your nose and from your abdomen as deeply as you can and hold your breath for a count of ten [Put your hand on your abdomen to make sure it is expanding as you breathe in, like a balloon would]
- Place your tongue between your front teeth and the roof of your mouth
- Slowly breathe out through your mouth. [As you breathe out, your abdomen should contract back in]
- Breathe out as long as you can so that you empty all the air [Short, anxious breathing is caused by shallow breathing in the upper cavity only]
- Repeat this as many times as you choose.

2.  Stress Relief: If you are under stress or need to relax quickly:
    - Place your arms down along the sides of your body
    - As you inhale deeply, stretch your arms up and out as if to form a V shape
    - Then exhale slowly through your mouth and bring your arms back down to your side
    - Repeat this as many times as you feel necessary
3.  Deep Breathing:
    - Empty your lungs by exhaling (pull in your stomach as you exhale)
    - Take a deep breath in (your stomach expands)
    - Hold breath for twice as long as it took to breathe in
    - Exhale for 4 times as long as it took to breathe in
    - Do this 8-10 times

D.  Body Inventory & Relaxation

There are times when we hold our muscles tight because of stress or busyness. In the Body Inventory we are purposefully relaxing our body so that it can cooperate in the Quieting Process. Here is the process:

- Move into a relaxed position, uncrossing your legs and arms
- Then starting with your toes, lightly squeeze them for 5 seconds and then release the squeeze
- Continue doing this with all your body parts as you continue to move up your body: legs, backside/hips, fingers/hands, arms, stomach, shoulders, neck, lips, and eyes [This will help in the relaxation of your muscles]

E. The Jesus Prayer
- The Jesus Prayer is based on the words of blind Bartimaeus, "Son of David, have mercy on me" (Mark 10:46-52). It can also be said as "Lord Jesus Christ, Son of God, have mercy on me a sinner" or even shortened to Jesus Christ have mercy on me.
- Whatever version you choose, repeat it a number of times and even coordinate it with your breathing. (This is done by inwardly saying part of it as you breathe in and the rest of it as you breathe out.)
- The Jesus Prayer can help your mind focus on one thing instead of a lot of racing thoughts. It can help quiet your mind.

The Jesus Prayer has sometimes been called, The Prayer of The Heart. It can also be helpful as a method of opening the heart and is considered to be the Unceasing Prayer that the apostle Paul advocated in the New Testament (II Thess. 5:17).

F. Imagery
- Imagery uses our imagination which helps to anchor our thoughts and focus our attention which is helpful in quieting our heart.[35]
- Here are some ideas for the use of imagery: Focus on Christ and image yourself in his presence. Or with eyes closed, image Christ within you. Or imagine his smile on you as stated in the book of Numbers, "May the Lord smile on you" (Num. 6:25, NLT).

- It can also be helpful to imagine a peaceful place that you have seen or been to before. Place yourself back in that place and even imagine Jesus being there with you.

## G. Aromatherapy

- It has been discovered that certain herbs have a calming type effect on us. Because of that, they can be beneficial for alleviating the tension inside of us, which can help reduce the stress we are feeling and help prepare us as we quiet our hearts.
- Chamomile and lavender seem to be effective for calming a person. They can help settle us down as we begin our time with God.
- Frankincense is considered the holy anointing oil in the Middle East, where it has been used in religious ceremonies for thousands of years. It was the oil that the Wise Men brought as a gift to Jesus and was one of the ingredients in the perfume of the sanctuary (Exo. 30:34). It has both comforting and stimulating qualities. The warm balsamic aroma is stimulating and can help focus our mind. It is also comforting and calming which can help as we meditate.
- Peppermint is said to calm one's digestion, improving one's comfort. Spearmint is said to offer us a sense of balance and well being.
- Lemon balm can also be stimulating, offering some extra assistance in focusing our mind.

- You can find these herbs in teas, room mists, essential oils, and candles. You can even grow your own fresh herbs.

## H. Other Helps

1. Prayer Shawl. The Greek word for closet is (*tameion*), which means an inner chamber, or a secret room. The use of a prayer shawl can remind us of the closet or private room Jesus referred to when he talked about prayer (Matt. 6:6, KJV).
   - The Prayer Shawl can be wrapped around you or placed over you as a reminder that Christ is surrounding you with his 'everlasting arms' (Deut. 33:27).
   - It is also warm and comforting and can create a sense of being concealed away from things around you.
2. A clinging cross. This cross is created out of wood and was made for the shape of anyone's hand. It can be helpful in sensing God's presence and a reminder that he is always with you. It is also symbolic of his sacrifice on the cross for you.
3. Light a candle. Sometimes it can be helpful to light a candle at the beginning of your time with God. The fire of a candle is calming to watch and it can remind us "Jesus is the light of the world" (Jn. 9:5). If you choose to light a candle regularly, it can provide a helpful way to signal to your mind and heart that you are beginning to spend time with God.

These suggestions are not meant to be a substitute for being with God or a magical tool. They are simply ways to help prepare you to be in God's presence. Many of them have biblical roots.

I have found the best way to enter God's presence with a peaceful and undistracted heart is to begin my time when I first get up in the morning. This happens before I turn on my computer, talk on the phone, or engage in work. Once I begin other activities, my mind tends to become distracted.

For me, this allows God to get the best time of my day since I am a morning person. But each person will need to decide when to spend time with God. The highest priority is to spend quality time with God no matter when that happens.

# Appendix B

## How to Enhance your Relationship with God: Clearing out the Debris

As we live life, we gather debris (clutter, toxins, junk, and gunk) and it hinders our body, soul, and spirit from being connected with God. It is important to plan times for clearing out the debris.

You will realize this is necessary when you notice a number of clues:

- Lack of spiritual appetite or feeling distant from God (You are not spending much time with God.)
- Busyness habit (You are always in a hurry, you are unable to be silent or still, or you are unable to quiet your heart.)
- Relationship Issues (You are experiencing conflicts, disagreements, arguments, and frequent irritability with other people in your life.)
- Emotional Consequences (You notice overtiredness, a feeling of being drained, emotional fatigue, burnout, brain fog, irritability, or a sense of being over-extended.)

These are signals that tell us that we need to attend to issues in our body, soul, and spirit. Otherwise, these issues will clog up the pathway to our relationship with God and make us more vulnerable to the enemy.

Here are some ways to deal with the debris that has gathered in our life:

1. Soul Care
   - Soul detox (allow God to reveal lies you are believing, heal the hurts in your life, forgive you for sins that he reveals, forgive people you have hurt and those who have hurt you)
   - Practice a daily Examen (see Appendix C)
   - Spend time in silence and quiet reflection
   - Simplify your life (get rid of the clutter and excess things in your home and schedule, which makes for a calmer mind and more peaceful soul)
   - See my book, *Formed Holy in his Image*, for more ideas on Soul Care.

2. Spirit Care
   - Media fast (fast for a day or more from all types of media – computer, iPad, TV, movies, social media like Facebook, internet, radio, smart phone activities and Apps, newspapers, magazines, etc.) Notice how you feel when you are without these things in your life
   - Spend more time in God's presence being silent in order to listen to him
   - Allow God's Word to reveal how he

- wants you to grow in him (Consider doing *Lectio Divina* or some other type of spiritual formation exercise every day; see Appendix C for additional ideas)
- Find an accountability partner or a small group to help in supporting your spiritual desire to grow closer to God
- Journal your thoughts, feelings, and longings
- Practice an attitude of gratitude and thankfulness

3. Body Care
- Attend to Body needs (prioritize getting more rest, taking time to walk or other exercise that you enjoy, drinking more water, and doing a cleanse)
- Light Cleanse (cut out caffeine, sugar, and junk foods for a period of time)
- Medium Cleanse (cut out the things in the light cleanse, as well as, non-healthy starches like white bread, white rice, white pasta, all sugar products, dairy and meat for a several days; try drinking more fresh juices, healthy protein drinks, and more fresh fruits and vegetables)
- Serious Cleanse (Fast for a day or more from all foods and drinks except water.) Make

sure you drink plenty of water during this type of cleanse. Try adding fresh lemon to it.

4. The acronym H.A.L.T.

- This is a reminder of red flags that can make you vulnerable to poor choices, bad decisions, and poor attitudes, which can also hinder your progress.

H – Hungry
A – Angry
L – Lonely
T – Tired

- When you sense one of these four concerns, it is time to stop (H.A.L.T.) so that you can take care of the issue. Usually there is a deeper issue under the concern that God may want to reveal to you.

# Appendix C

## Other Spiritual Formation Exercises that Engage the Mind & Heart

1. Praying the Scriptures (by Madame Guyon)

*Don't just skim the surface; plunge deeply within to grasp it all!*

- Choose a passage that is simple & fairly practical *(this will usually be a small portion of Scripture)*
- Come quietly and humble to the Lord *(silence your heart)*
- Read slowly the passage of Scripture *(meditate on the words and do not move from one line to another until you have sensed the heart of what you have read)*
- Take a portion of the scripture that has touched you and turn it into a prayer *(or turn each line into a prayer once you have sensed the heart of it)*

2. Spending Time with Christ (Gospel Meditation)

*A gospel meditation provides an opportunity for you to enter specific moments in Jesus' life and share his experience.*

- Select a Gospel account of one event in the life of Christ
- Begin with a brief prayer asking God to help you enter this story and encounter Jesus
- Read the scripture slowly as you observe the situation presented

- Watch, listen & stay attentive to Christ, not the other people in the story *(just be present to Jesus)*
- Don't try to analyze the story or learn its lessons *(what did you discover about Jesus as you shared this experience with him?)*

3. Sitting in God's Presence (by Basil Pennington)

- Simply shut your eyes and enjoy the presence of the Lord
- Focus on Christ as he gazes back at you with his full loving attention and asks you to sit with him for a while
- Gently return your attention to him by saying his name whenever you find your mind drifting to other things

4. Breath Prayer

*(Combines calming effect of breath with words of Scripture)*

- Get seated comfortably and began slowly breathing
- Begin inwardly saying a phrase of scripture in rhythm with your breathing.

For instance:

Breathe in: The Lord...

Breathe out: ...is my Shepherd

- Focus during every repetition on the meaning of the words, praying them from the heart and in the heart.

## 5. Daily Examen

*This can help increase your awareness of God.*

- Take a few minutes to prayerfully review your day and what took place
- Reflect or do these things:
  When did God feel closest to you today?
  When did he seem absent?
  Ask God forgiveness for a sin or ask someone to
      forgive you
  Thank God for his presence.

## 6. Experiencing the Heart of God
   [A method by Thom Gardner[36]]

- Still your thoughts and emotions as you center your thoughts on Christ
- Meditate on a verse of scripture, saying it softly over and over to yourself until you can say it (or a portion of it) with your eyes closed
- As you repeat the scripture allow yourself to see it with the eyes of your heart
- Journal your response to these questions:
  - ✓ *What is the picture you see in your mind's eye as you repeat the scripture?*
  - ✓ *What does the scripture reveal about heart of God?*
  - ✓ *Put yourself in the picture of this scripture in your mind. What is the Lord speaking to you personally as you see the truth of this scripture?*
- Prayerfully tell God what you have seen and heard today through this experience.

# Appendix D

## Other Books by the Author

Formed Holy in his Image: Spirit, Soul and Body, 2011.

Turning OFF Noise; Tuning IN to Health Sound, 2010.

Peace in Anxious Times: A Holistic Approach, 2016

## Author's Personal Website

www.gwenebner.com

# Endnotes

1. Parker Palmer, "Teaching Poetry with Lectio Divina," www.mikeruso.com/blog/teaching-poetry-with-lectio-divina/ [accessed October 11, 2016].

**Chapter 1**
2. Henri Nouwen, *Heart Speaks to Heart* (Notre Dame, IN: Ava Marie Press, 1989), 51.

3. Charles Ringma, *Dare to Journey with Henri Nouwen* (Colorado Springs: Pinon Press, 2000), Reflection 5.

4. St. Augustine, *"Confessions of St. Augustine,"* (Simon & Brown, 2012).

5. Maggie and Duffy Robbins, *Enjoy the Silence* (Grand Rapids, MI: Zondervan, 2005), 10.

6. Mary Margaret Funk, *Tools Matter for Practicing the Spiritual Life* (New York, NY: Continuum, 2001), 11.

7. Ibid., 9.

8. Ibid., 12.

9. Ibid., 13.

10. Ibid., 14.

11. Ibid., 10.

12. American Psychological Association, "The left brain knows what the right hand is doing," http://www.apa.org/monitor/2009/01/ brain.aspx [accessed July 2, 2013].

13. Ask.com, "Psychology: Left brain vs. Right brain," http://psychology.about.com/od/cognitivepsychology/a/left -brain-right-brain.htm [accessed July 2, 2013].

14. Ibid.

15. Some typical careers that might be more left-brained oriented are computer programming, salesperson, paralegal, health care, banker, judge, mathematician, librarian, accountant, lab scientist, lawyer, building inspector, administrator, financial planner, and engineer.

16. Richard Foster, *Celebration of Discipline* (Downers Grove, IL: InterVarsity Press, 1978, 1988), 15.

17. Thomas à Kempis, *The Imitation of Christ* (Garden City, NY: Image Books, 1955), 85.

18. Foster 1988, 20.

19. Richard Foster, *Sanctuary of the Soul: Journey into Meditative Prayer* (Downers Grove, IL: InterVarsity Press, 2011), 35-36.

20. Ibid.

21. Ibid., 2.

22. A.W. Tozer, "The Value of the Sanctified Imagination" (a series of essays by A.W. Tozer) http://www.christianimagination.com/2012/02.28/tozer-the-value-of-a-sanctified-imagination/ [accessed October 11, 2016].

23. If you are interested in more information on meditation, I would suggest you read Richard Foster's book, *Sanctuary of the Soul: Journey into Meditative Prayer*.

**Chapter 2**
24. Romero de Lima Gouvea, "Lectio Divina," http://www.carmelite.org/documents/Spirituality/rdlglecti odivina.pdf [accessed October 15, 2016].

25. Tony Jones, *The Sacred Way* (Grand Rapids, MI: Zondervan, 2005), 51.

26. Hugh Feiss, *Essential Monastic Wisdom: Writings on the Contemplative Lifestyle* (San Francisco: Harper, 1999), 21.

27. Michael Casey, *Sacred Reading: The Ancient Art of Lectio* (Liguori, Missouri: Liguori Publications, 1997), 83.

28. Ibid.

29. This came from a seminar with Thom Gardner called, "Restored Life Seminar".

30. Contemplative Outreach, *"About Lectio,"* http://www.centeringprayer.com/lectio_divina.html [accessed June 19, 2013].

31. Jones, 54.

32. Foster 1988, 27.

33. Maggie and Duffy Robbins, *Enjoy the Silence* (Grand Rapids, MI: Zondervan, 2005), 16.

**Appendix A**
34. Adele Ahlberg Calhoun, *Spiritual Disciplines Handbook: Practices that Transform Us*. (Downers Grove, IL: InterVarsity Press, 2005), 50. I have adjusted her exact procedure for the *lectio* experience.

35. Foster 2011, 35-36.

**Appendix C**
36. Thom Gardner, *Healing the Wounded Heart* (Shippensburg, PA: Destiny Image Publishers, 2005).

# ~ NOTES or JOURNAL ~

*"Now may the God of peace*
*make you holy in every way,*
*and may your whole*
***spirit and soul and body***
*be kept blameless until our Lord*
*Jesus Christ comes again.*
*God will make this happen,*
*For he who calls you is faithful."*

(I Thess. 5:23-24, NLT, bold added)